Spellbinders

SIGNS & WONDERS

D1516273

SIGNS & WONDERS

WRITER: Mike Carey

PENCILS: Mike Perkins

INKS: Drew Hennessy

COLORS: Guru eFX

LETTERS: VC's Randy Gentile

EDITOR: MacKenzie Cadenhead

CONSULTING EDITOR: Mark Paniccia

SPELLBINDERS CREATED BY
Mike Carey & Mike Perkins

COLLECTION EDITOR: Jennifer Grünwald

ASSISTANT EDITOR: Michael Short

SENIOR EDITOR, SPECIAL PROJECTS: Jeff Youngquist

DIRECTOR OF SALES: David Gabriel

BOOK DESIGNER: Carrie Beadle

CREATIVE DIRECTOR: Tom Marvelli

EDITOR IN CHIEF: Joe Quesada

PUBLISHER: Dan Buckley

Ouch. A little wide of the *mark* there.

You think this is *funny*, Paul? Knox *died* last night.

And his mom and dad won't even *know*. They'll think he ran *away* or something.

Renata

Paul

Mason

Yeah, but it *could* be worse--because it could be *me*.

Like I *told* you, Mason, Foley asked me first. Only I had the *sense* to say no.

The weird thing is *how* he died. He was a *life-lender*, right?

It's like his own power *short-circuited*. You're coming up to the *ten-minute* mark here.

Thanks, Ren.

At least someone's got a sense of priorities.

So, what was Foley up to, anyway?

What, you haven't heard him do his thing?

The sky's gonna fall, the seas are gonna boil, and the heavens will rain fire on the junior prom?

He wants to summon some kind of *über-mage* to whip all of us true-born Salemites into *shape.*

Some sort of "Sabrina Joins the *Marine* Corps" deal.

Freaky. So--you think they *did* it?

Found a *super-witch* and reeled 'im in?

Well *Foley* was doing the asking, and Knox ended up spread over the *landscape.*

Bets?

Barrow

I'm Chad *Barrow*. I live across the *street*.

Boy, your *dad's* sure got a lot of tools.

Hi.

Oh, these are *mine*. I do a lot of--

Heavy *engineering*?

--sculpture. It's kind of a *hobby*. I'm--

You're Kim *Vesco*. You just drove in from *Chicago*. And tomorrow is your first *day* at John Hathorne High School.

O-o-okay.

I thought those were *my* lines, but I'm happy to just stand here and *listen*.

Sorry. They put a *notice* up saying we should all welcome you to the *school* and to Massachusetts.

They did *what?* You're putting me *on.*

Nope. You really *sculpt* with a chainsaw?

In my *old* school, that would've been like putting a *sign* around my neck that said "roll me and leave me for *dead.*"

Nah, JH²S is *okay.* Mostly.

So long as you're not a nerd or a *wick.*

A nerd or a *who?*

Oops, my *bad.* Look, I don't even *care* about that stuff.

Just keep your *head* down until you get the hang of the place, and you'll do *fine.*

See you *tomorrow,* Kim.

Yeah. Tomorrow.

"I can hardly *wait...*"

Mink

Liza Beth

First *impressions?*

Just the *obvious* one: I think Foley's *full* of it.

But in case he *isn't,* keep your eyes open.

So *that's* the new girl.

Well Chicago's main export is raw *meat.*

Oh my god, *look* at this. Foley's gonna say *hello* to her or something.

Talk about the kiss of *death.*

Listen, you're--

I'm *sorry?*

I think that-- you could be--

I can't *hear* you.

Well, I suppose I'll *overlook* the late arrival of Miss Vesco.

Provided she can tell us why Prague's *Hunger* Wall is so called.

ters 13'

Totally got *pounded* by an air elemental.

Bummer!

Is she a *wick* or something? 'Cause I heard--

Claro que le daremos a Kim un gran bienvenido *bilingüe* de John Hathorne High School.

Todos juntos.

BIENVENIDA KIM

--seems to be all friendly with *FrankenFoley.*

Then she's *gotta* be a wick.

She's gotta be sick in the *head,* is what.

No, no! Try to *feel* it. Try to feel the *tragedy* of it.

"The heavens *themselves* blaze *forth* the *death* of princes!"

She got *chomped* on by a suckbag?

Yeah, her!

Man, what do they *teach* them in Chicago?

SCIENCE

LANGUAGES

CAFETARIA

LIBRARY

So what's your *lineage*?

Huh?

Y'know, where do you *place* on the pillar of *smoke*?

Okay, that must be an East *Coast* kind of thing.

Because I don't have the *faintest* idea what you're *talking* about.

Oh, ri-i-ight. You've already made friends with *Foley* and his little bunch of *losers.*

What?

Well, enjoy your stay in the *leper* colony.

Outstanding, girl.

At the risk of *repeating* myself--

What?

The wicks and the *sparkle-hags* have it all their own *way* around here. It's *great* that you told Mason where to get *off*.

Yeah, that was pure *style*, Kim. I wish I could watch it again in *slo-mo*.

Listen, I'm having a *party* on Saturday--no wicks allowed. You've *got* to come.

BRRRRRRRRRING

Oops, better *run*.

Maybe they don't even *have* wicks in Chicago.

No, the *gangsters* gunned 'em all down!

Okay, I *am* gonna freak. But I'm gonna pick my *own* time and place.

What? Hey, what does *that* mean? And who is *he*?

Do you know what's going *on* here? Come *back*!

Come *back* to us, darling.

Oh *please*, Kim! Come *back* to us!

Wh--? Oh, *great*!

This bites! This *really* bites!

GUUUH!

Kim! Oh, *baby*!

What *happened* to you?

I just--fell and hit my *head*, mom. Nothing *serious.*

Nothing *serious*? Sweetheart, you were out *cold* there.

It's *my* fault. I was so excited to get up here. I pushed us all too *hard.*

Yeah. *That* must be it.

Foley wants us to *what?* No, no! Don't say it *again*, Paul! I'm *eating!*

He wants *our* coven to team up with *his.*

Is he *on* something? I mean, he's hitting zero for *three.*

First he tells us the *sky's* gonna fall, and it *doesn't.*

Second, he gets Knox *killed* with his stupid *summoning* spell.

And *third*-- what was third?

The *Vesco* kid. He said she was the *über-witch* he was trying to summon.

Right-- and she's just a *blank.*

Hey, Ren. Are you in the *world?*

Hello?

Huh?

Sorry. My *pancake's* got the number of the *Beast* burned through it.

You think that's an *omen* or something?

You're late *again*, Miss Vesco. Are you still on *Chicago* time?

No, I was--umm--sort of *sick*. I've got a *note*.

I see. You fell and hit your *head*, and your parents took you to the *hospital* for a check-up.

Well, I'll expect you to catch up on the *notes* you've missed. Take your *seat*.

The *hospital*? Are you *okay*, Kim?

I hope you can still come to my *party* on Saturday night.

Yeah, *sure* I can. I'm *fine*, Kris. Honest.

Does she *know* what that looks like? A *witch* hanging with blanks?

If she even *is* a witch.

She's--you've gotta *trust* me, LB. She's the one we--she's--

Knox *died* for this.

You've gotta *trust* me.

Hey, back off, okay? School's the last place we want to be talking about--

No, it's all *right*, Mink. I'll--I *want* to explain. I think it's-- I think she's *right*.

Look at *that*, Mason. She's breaking up the happy *home*.

Barrow, as far as I'm concerned, Kim Vesco is an un-person. Now will you *please* boil that water?

Okay, I'll try to *explain*.

Can you *look* at me while you do it?

No. I *can't*.

Because you're gonna *lie* to me?

Because I've got a-- you know, a--a *condition*.

I can't-- it's not--I don't--when I try to--

Okay, I *get* it.

Eye contact is *optional*. Just spit it out.

Salem is kind of a-- it's an *unusual* place. There are--

People around here--*families* around here--they can use *magic*. Some of them.

Families?

Yeah, it-- *runs* in families. You get--you don't *learn* spells. There are spells *in* you.

And it's like--each family always gets the *same* kind of magic.

We came here from-- we lived somewhere else. That's the story.

Something called the--the Thief came and--it's--we couldn't fight it. We had to come here. To Salem.

And where do *I* fit in?

I was having *dreams* about--like, the end of the *world*.

And there was this one witch who could *stop* it.

So I--I did a *summoning* spell.

And *you* came.

Are you putting me *on?* Man, I can't stop *traffic!*

I'm not even a--whatever *you* guys are. No magic wand, no pointy hat. Get it?

So you think they're gonna close **school** for the day?

At John *Hathorne*?

I'm amazed they didn't make us finish out the *lesson*.

Hey, Kim.

Hey, Barrow-- Chad.

Here. It's hot *chocolate*-- good for *shock*.

So what did you do up there? And how come you smell of... umm... *fertilizer*?

I made a *mora poultice*.

A *what*?

You know I do *sculptures*, right? You've seen my *rig*.

A poultice is mostly *ammonium* salts and baking powder. You use it to *clean* stone and metal.

But it's the same stuff they drop from planes onto *forest* fires.

Never thought I'd use it to save my *life*. Funny, huh?

Hey, this *happens*, you know? The witches fight among themselves and *we* get caught in the *crossfire*.

Innocent *Bystander* High?

Exactly.

One reason why witches don't make class *president* all that often.

Umm-- on a *lighter* note--if you don't have anyone to go to Kris Cabot's *party* with--

You're asking me for a *date*? After all this-- stuff?

Yeah. Bad *timing*, right?

Perfect timing. A date sounds so--normal. Like what *sane* people do! Yeah, I'd *love* to go with you.

Great. You'll have a good *time*, Kim. It's blanks only. There won't be any of this *wick* stuff going on.

I'll pick you up at *seven* on Saturday, okay?

No, I'll come over to *your* house.

But won't your *parents* prefer it if I--?

My *adoptive* parents. You'll get to meet them sooner or later. Let's make it *later*.

You're--

--adopted?

She's *what?*

Well, that's the story that's going *around.*

Look, I know you think Foley *OD'ed* on stupid pills, LB, but hear me *out.*

There *is* some weird stuff going down. And someone does seem to be trying to *whack* Vesco.

And I was thinking--Kris Cabot's party, that's *guaranteed* to be a witch-free *zone.*

Now if Vesco is *adopted,* she could be from *Salem.* She could be one of *us.*

So Foley could be *right* about her being *important* in some--

Yeah, yeah. I don't need the *Cliff's* notes.

Fine. I'll put a *blessing* on her, okay?

Hey, who'd *believe* it? Chicago was *adopted...*

"I wonder how *wide* the choice was at *that* orphanage?"

How are we going to fit the *desk* into that tiny space?

I don't *know*, Pat. Shave off the *sides*? Fold it up like an *accordion*?

Hi, darling. Good day at *school*?

Science lab blew up.

It was *fine* apart from that.

Have you noticed how she uses *sarcasm* to avoid answering questions she doesn't *like*?

Yes.

I wonder where she gets *that* from.

Y	SATURDAY	SUNDAY
	1 PARTY AT KRIS'S- 7.00 CHAD.	2
	8	9

Kiiim! I'm so glad you could *make* it!

And I *love* what you're wearing. Did you bring it with you from *Chicago*?

There's *nowhere* to shop around here except Lili and My Simon.

How'd you and *Chad* get so friendly? Is there something we should *know*?

He lives across the *street* from me.

And that's *all*?

Kris, I've known him for, like, six *days*--

Yeah, but "still *waters*", y'know? Barrow's *way* deep.

Where *is* Chad, anyway? We just walked in and he *disappeared*.

The *game*.

The *game*?

Pats are playing the New York something-or-others. Serves me *right* for not checking the date.

The guys were gonna *riot* if I didn't turn on the *widescreen* in the den.

But anyway, that's *cool*. It means they can't *complain* if we do some *girl* stuff.

Well, I should tell him I'm--what *kind* of stuff?

Not *nails* and *hair*?

Come on, no one's gonna miss us!

So what do you *think*? Be *honest.*

Better yet, be *envious.*

Krissy, it's *gorgeous!* Is this for the *Saturnalia?*

Is the Pope *papal?*

The *Saturnalia?* What's *that?*

It's just this *thing* the school puts on in the Spring semester. Like, a *sports* day and then a *talent* show afterwards.

It's *very* cool, Kim. You're gonna *love* it.

Hey! Kris, is there anyone *else* up--?

PHUTT

Oh, great. I'll have to go reset the *breakers* in the basement.

No.

I don't think you should *do* that.

Well, I--I don't think I *should.* I mean, you don't even *know* me. We only just--

I know you're the most beautiful girl I ever *saw.*

What *else* is there to know?

Well, oka-ay. I live on Fairfax. 1103 *Fairfax.*

That's great. I'll see you *later.*

Uh-- what was your *name* again?

Ren, this is *stupid.* Just because the new kid is *accident-prone--*

Mason, Kim was *attacked* by an air elemental. And the science lab blew up around her *ears.*

If someone sets you on *fire,* you don't go "what a crummy *accident"!* Foley says--

I *know* what Foley says. She's the *über-witch.* She's gonna *save* us all.

Truth? She's a *blank* who never should've let go of mommy's *hand.*

Maybe. But in case you're *wrong,* I asked L.B. to put a *blessing* on her.

I don't want anything to *happen* when we're not around to step *in.*

Liza Beth *blessed* her?

Sure she did. And I mean *tight*.

What, the whole *works*?

Triple ward. She wiped herself right *out*. No magics can *touch* Kim now.

Cool. What if someone smashes her skull in with a *brick*?

Wh-- what?

Come on, Ren, it's just *tunnel* vision. What's to stop someone attacking her with a *mundane* weapon?

Or with their bare--?

Stupid! Stupid, stupid, stupid!

Ren, wait! Don't just run off by *yourself!*

Chill, Mason. We'll bring up the *rear*.

After all--

--it's not like I could keep up.

What happened to the *lights*?

Never mind the *lights*, what happened to the *game*?

Kris! Hey, Kris! Where are the *fuses*?

They're probably down in the *basement*. You'll need a *flashlight*, Wendell.

I *won't* need a--

AH! AH! AH!

KZZZZZZZT!

Wendellllllll!

Don't *touch* him! He's still *live*!

Did that look like *electricity* to you?

Wh-- what are we gonna--?

Let's get *out* of here!

Don't *leave* me! Don't *leave* me!

Someone call the *police*!

"Why can't she *stay* blessed?"

He's only a few feet *away* from you.

Over by the *stairs*.

You sure pick your *times*, dead girl.

No, I think it's *you*. I think *you* pick my times.

What?

You don't know what you *are* yet, do you? But you know what you can *do*.

So you should *do* it. You don't have anything to *lose*.

Yes! That's it! It's like--your body is an *egg*--

...--and the shell is *cracking!*

Well, that was a *lot* easier than last time.

Yeah. I think you'll get better and *better* at it.

Look at this guy.

Kkkhhhhh!

You think you've got me *pinned*, don't you, you sick *freak?*

I wish I could pull that stupid *mask* off your face and find out who you *are.*

But I guess I've got some *other* options.

What are you going to *do?*

Watch me.

WHUMP

UKKK!

I'm not--

I'm just not *getting* this. Any of it!

Doesn't *surprise* me. I mean, you've got that whole naïve *charm* thing going.

Zip it, Mason.

You want to try zipping it *for* me, L.B.?

Happy to. So long as *pretty* boy here doesn't try to fill me with love and *peace*.

Oww!

Hey, come *on*, guys!

Foley, you *still* think Kim is a witch?

Yeah. I do.

And that she's gonna--I dunno--*save* us all from something?

Yeah.

But you can't tell us from *what?* Or *when?* Or *how?*

No. I can't--I didn't *see* that. I'm sorry.

Oh, no *problem.*

So--is there any chance you could be from *Salem?*

I don't *know* where I'm from.

I grew up in an *orphanage*, okay?

What's to *tell*? The witch families of Salem-- they're refugees. They came here from somewhere *else*, okay?

At least, that's the *story*. And they brought the pillar *with* them, because it was precious. They didn't wanna leave it *behind*.

N--nobody remembers what it --what the thief was, any more. But the pillar is--is--kind of a magical litmus paper.

It *tells* you what you are-- and it brings out your *power*.

Every witch kid gets to *touch* it when they're about *five*.

Thanks for the *exposition*.

But I'm not *going*.

What? But don't you want to *know* if you're a *wick* or not?

I really *appreciate* you all bailing me out tonight. But a dead girl told me *not* to go. And I *trust* her.

If you see Chad *Barrow*, tell him I went *home*.

A *dead* girl told her.

I caught that too.

Wonder if it's anyone we *know*.

Mom! Dad! What *happened?*

Oh, Kim! We only stepped *out* for a walk!

We were gone for twenty *minutes,* tops.

Then we came *back,* and--

Oh no.

--and the *door* was open--

Oh *no!*

All my *work.* All my *tools.*

Sweetheart, I'm so *sorry.*

Everything.

We'll do what we *can.* Some of your pieces--

Well, maybe we can *fix* them.

Yeah. Dad, just-- give me a *second,* will you?

TEK TEK TEK

Yeah, a *Salem* number, please. Lowell. *Renata* Lowell.

Thanks.

Hey, Ren. It's *me*.
Kim Vesco.

When you get this, *call* me.
I changed my *mind*.
If I've got any witch powers coming to me, I want them *now*.

Let's *do* this.

Oh, *yeah*.

Let's.

"Pillar of Smoke". Why is it even *called* that?

Duh! Because that's what it *is*, Kim.

Some of the time, anyway. Not *always*.

Oh, great *explanation*, Mink! Really gets to the *point*.

The thing *is*, Vesco, Salem witches *came* here from someplace *else*.

We don't know *where*, or why, except that they were *running* from something.

The *Thief*.

Hey, you *had* your turn.

They brought the pillar of smoke *with* them. In the same way you'd take a *cannon* with you when you left a battlefield.

A *cannon*? What kind of a dumb--?

Y'know, so the enemy don't get a *hold* of it and turn it on *you*.

Anyway, we should *get* there before night. Then you'll *see*.

Before *night*? Geez, when do we get *home* again? We've got *school* tomorrow.

No problem. *Mason* will take care of that.

After we've *touched* the pillar, our batteries will be *way* charged.

I'll have enough magic to *travel* us all home to Salem.

CLICK Quick as *that*.

"Every soul on *evil* bent, from our pathway *interdict.*"

Good idea, L.B.

Yeah, thanks. I really need *your* approval.

Walk *around* the blessing, okay?

There's no way I'm drawing it *again* if you mess it up.

Now--what am I seeing here, L.B.?

Does this mean I'm not welcome or something?

Nah, it's okay. I know you didn't mean it.

Okay, give the guy some *room.* You know he *hates* being crowded.

I don't-- I can't even *see* him today. Wonder if he's--y'know--asleep.

Yeah, *right,* Foley. The guardian's *asleep.*

The *guardian?* Are we *meeting* someone here?

What, are you blind, Vesco?

Oh my g--

Hey, do we *have* to go through this whole "three billy goats *gruff*" thing every time we come up here?

It's *us*, Kally. Give us a *break*, yeah?

I do not *know* this one.

I--I'm-- I--my name is--

Rik a tik a tik, *Sliiiim shady.*

And she is *not* of the bloodlines.

Yes she *is*, Apocaledon. She's never touched the *pillar*, is all. She's like a baby is, before the ritual.

This is no *baby*. She is almost *grown*.

Her folks never *brought* her here. Can't you let us *vouch* for her?

GRRRRMMM!

I like it *not*. But if *you* speak for her, Liza Beth--

You're a *sweetheart*, Kally.

Here. See what *Santa's* brought you.

This is a day of ill *omen*. The air smells of *blood* not yet spilled--

Ahhh, *Snickers!* Excellent!

What *was* that thing?

The *guardian.* When the first-- when the *witches* came to Salem--

--they *put* him here to protect the *pillar.*

We're too *early.* We'll have to *wait* a half hour or so.

We shouldn't get *close* to it until it reaches the *cusp.*

The cusp of *what?*

It's going to *change.* From smoke into *fire.*

If a *witch* approaches it then, and *sweet-talks* it a little, it turns into *stone* instead.

Then you can *touch* it.

And then I'll-- become a *witch?*

Yeah, with a pointy *hat* and everything. Tchah.

You'll *wake up* to your power. Whatever's *inside* you will come out.

You mean she's gonna *barf?*

Great. Maybe we should *film* it and sell *copies.*

Hey, Ren. Did any of you guys know a girl named *Sally*? Chad *Barrow's* girlfriend?

Sally *Shearman*? Sure, we knew her. Why?

Well, how did she *die*?

Wow. You just come right *out* with it, don't you?

Oh, I'm *sorry*. I didn't mean to--

It's okay. She was kind of in my *coven* for a while, that's all. No *big*.

I didn't even know she was a *witch*.

She was a *salamander*.

Means she could *do* stuff with heat and *cold*.

Mainly toast *marshmallows* and chill *beer*.

Sally was totally on *space* biscuits! Never took *anything* seriously.

Least, till she started fetching sticks for that *blank*, Barrow.

Then she *stopped* doing magic because it made him *tense*. Feh.

So was her death-- y'know--an *accident*?

Maybe. Hard to *say*, really. She *froze* to death.

Last *August*.

Like *Knox*?

What?? Knox turned into *lizards*.

Yeah, but I mean, his own *magic* killed him. That's what you *said*.

Maybe this is some kind of--I dunno, a *disease* that witches get.

What am I *hearing*? You think this is "Let's Host a *Mystery*" or something?

You're here five *minutes*, and you're telling *us* what's going on?

Wait a minute, Mason. I think--God, why didn't I *see* that?

A witch *disease*? Are you joking?

Not that, but Kim's right that it's our *own* magic that's being used *against* us.

Think about it.

Mink was in the science lab when Mister X threw that *curse*. I was around when he turned into a *wolf*.

But at Kris Cabot's *party*-- where there were *no* witches at all--he had to go after Kim with a *knife*. It fits.

That's the stupidest thing I ever *heard*.

What, because it's someone *else's* idea, it's got to be *bad*? Get over yourself, Mason.

Hey, come on, LB--

Stay *out* of it, Mink. If we're lucky they'll *mud wrestle*.

L--look! Look!

Ap-- Apo--

Oh help me, help me.

It's the *big, bad wolf.*

Oh pillar of smoke, I-- we need to do the *thing*--the *ritual*.

We're-- I've--we have to--

There's a *witch* here who wants to know what she *is*. Please?

Go right up *close*. One of the sigils will start to-- to *shine*.

That one's *yours*. Touch it, and you'll *know*. Your power will--

--you'll *see*.

Chad. I-- I thought--

What? That we had a *thing*?

Sorry, babe. I've already *got* a girlfriend.

In fact, that's what *all* this is really *about*.

That's why I had to *come* here. Why I had to *make* you show me the way.

Of course, *witch* kids get to touch the pillar when they're about a month *old*.

Then why didn't--?

Because I'm *not* a witch.

Are you a little *slow*, or something?

The bloodlines don't always breed *true*. Sometimes there's a *mutation*.

That's what the *Thief* was. That's what I am. Any magic that's around me, I can suck it up like a *sponge*.

Exhibit number *one*.

Frankenfoley's magic *radar*--

--I can borrow *that* whenever the hell I need it.

UFF!

THE CHARMER

THE SACRIFICE

THE PILLAR

Okay, everyone get in *close*. I'm gonna travel us to the *Shaughnessy-Kaplan* Hospital.

I went there when my *knee* got whacked in that game against *Cambridge*. I think I can hit it.

Finally.

Come *on*, Mink. We're going *home*.

Okay, I was just-- Okay.

Hold on *tight*, yeah?

It could be a bumpy *ride*.

The--the sigil fell *apart*. I couldn't *hold* it!

I *told* you. Magic doesn't *work* right here.

Face it, Barrow had our *number*. He *played* us.

He made us *lead* him to the pillar, then he beat us till we *bled*.

"And now he's loose in *Salem*."

"And there isn't a single *thing* we can do about it."

Hey, Barrow, what's with the *lights*? And the school *bell*?

It's the middle of the *night*.

And you're *shining*. Is that magic? I thought you were a *blank*.

The lights and the bell don't *matter*, guys.

Don't *matter*? But they woke us up. They *made* us--

They're not what *brought* you here.

I brought you.

I called *out* to the Salem witches with the power of the pillar of *smoke*, and you were *closest*--

--so you get to be *first*.

B--Barrow! You can't--

Kim!

You're gonna have to wake *up*.

Come *on*, Kim.

I don't think you've got a lot of *time* left.

What--? Where--?

No!

Oh, th-- thank you, god! I'm--I thought you had *br--brain* damage or something.

Sally!

What?

Hi, Kim. I'm glad you're *okay*.

What do you *mean*, not much time? Where's *Barrow?*

I *told* you not to come here. *Look* at this.

He *smashed* the pillar of smoke. And he stole its *power*. He's become a *focus* for magic.

Uhh--maybe you *do* have a little--I mean, you should--

I came because he was trying to *kill* me.

I was trying to wake up my *own* magic.

Yeah. I *know*.

Call was *right*. Someone's breaking into the *school*.

Probably *kids* playing around.

Let's catch the little *scumbags* at it.

Hey. What are you *doing* there?

Did you break that *padlock*?

Shut up and be *stone* or something.

No, salt. Turn into *salt*.

Not *bad*. Not *enough* yet, but still. Not *half* bad.

No you're **not**, Mason. I think I know where we **are** now. I figured it out.

This is-- where the Salem witches **came** from. The world we left **behind** us.

The world that--?

--that we **surrendered** to the Thief. And this is what the Thief **did** to it.

Sucked it **dry** until there's nothing left except a--an open **wound,** that magic bleeds out of.

So how do we get **back?**

What do I look like, **Triple-A?** Maybe-- if LB does a blessing on **you**--if she can make it **stick** on you for just a second--

--it'll **shield** you--for, like, a count of **one.** And you'll be able to finish your **travel** spell.

But if this is the place the Thief chased us **out** of, then where **is** it?

Maybe it ran out of **magic** to eat, and then--

--kind of--**starved** to death?

Or maybe **not.**

Say *sorry* to the--?

Sally, there's nothing *there*. Barrow *smashed* the pillar into a million pieces.

He smashed the part that you can *see*.

But-- are you saying that--?

Everything has a *foundation*, Kim. The Pillar exists in *earth*, as well as in air.

Usually the *earth* part stays hidden. But some of the most *powerful* sigils of all are there.

This could be your last *chance* to find out what you are.

Please. *Forgive* us for what happened. We were careless, and we let Barrow *harm* you.

But if you'll *help* us, we can still--

Kim! I can't *see*!

What's *happening*?

Hang *on*, Foley! I think we got our *wish*.

I thought you said you were aiming for the *hospital.*

I was. But the *school* came into my head at the last moment. So *sue* me.

Who needs *hospitals?* I can do a proper *heal-all* now.

There's something *weird* going on. It's got to be *Monday* now, right?

So where *is* everyone?

You want some *water,* Ren? I'll get some from the *fountain.*

...

No! No!

Easy. Easy now. You're not *scared.*

You're just--you're *fine.* You're feeling *calmer* now.

He--he *took* them all. All the *witches.* He took them to the *gym.*

And then he locked the *doors.*

Okay. I'm gonna *do* this.

Wait! Wait for *me.*

I'm on my--I'm coming down.

Is something supposed to *happen?*

Am I supposed to *feel* something? Because I don't feel a--

--a--
--a--

AAAARRRGGHHH!

Kim!

This-- it's not like-- It doesn't usually--

HHHHHHHELP MMMMMEEEEE

Kim, I can't--I don't--I can't--

Neither can I, Foley. But let's keep it *together*, okay?

I got us in here. I'll get us *out*.

Oh no! That--that *thing* is--

It's *seen* us. It's coming this *way*!

I know. Try to look--*casual*.

What *make* you in this place? Why *move* you here?

We're just--*lost*, is all.

My name is Kim Vesco, and this is--

We *know* what you are, gatekeeper. But your *purpose* know we not.

Why move you here, when there is a breach in the *world*? Serve you not to *heal*?

Uh---say *what*?

Asrokhel speaks *truth*. She is *come* again.

In her glory. In her *living* flesh.

Homage to her. Love to her. Obeisance to her.

Hey, erase and *rewind*, guys. I need this in *English*.

You are the *necromancer*. You bind the *dead*, and set them free. You guard the *way*.

Okay. Any clues as to *why*?

Because someone *must*.

The *pillar* chooses one, in each age. Always the same one. *Different* always.

To guard the gate. To heal the *breaches* made by the mad and the *desperate*.

As *now*.

Do you not *feel* the hole in the world? The *wound* cut into life itself?

Not-- exactly.

You *will*. You must *go* there. But *you* only. To pass *back* through the gate is the gatekeeper's privilege.

He stays here. With the dead.

But I can sure make you *wish* you hadn't.

AAAAAA!

Curse. Transform. Travel.

Hey, let's make a *daisy* chain.

Man! Is there *anything* I can't do?

The *necromancer*, resign her duties?

The gatekeeper, *abandon* the gate?

Blasphemy!

You would *do* this thing? Defy your *destiny*, and the cosmic *balance*?

Inside of a New York *minute*, mister.

We both *stay*, or we both *go*. Believe.

Very well. We *submit* to the gatekeeper's will. As we *must*.

Well, that's *good*. --okay then. Fine.

Excellent.

Now take us to where this *breach* is at.

Like I can't *guess*.

The gate is *yours* to open and to close.

Your *mind* is the anvil on which our world is beaten out and *shaped*.

Then let there be-- --you know-- --a gate.

Oh wow! Get *over* here, Foley. The light's on *green*.

Go *well*, gatekeeper. Go *carefully*.

Thanks. But I don't think that's an *option*.

Kim. This hole-in-the-*world* th--thing. You think it's *Barrow*?

Of *course* it's Barrow. He's brought *Sally* back to life.

And I bet that isn't *all* he's done.

Foley, I've got a kind of an *idea*.

Means you may have to stand up to Barrow by *yourself* for a while, okay?

N--n--n--

Yeah. I suppose.

Then let's *go*.

Oh great. He travelled us off to some place *else* again.

Okay. Does anyone have the *slightest* idea where we are?

No. But it feels-- I don't know--like I *ought* to. Like I've been here *before*.

Maybe it's your *sock* drawer.

Can't be. We're still *alive*.

Well, can you travel us back to the *school*?

You think I'm not *trying*? Nothing's happening.

I'm running on *empty* here.

But there *is* magic here. Really strong. And all *around* us.

I don't *get* it.

I wonder if--man, that *would* be something.

Mink, that feeling of *déjà vu* you're getting--

Does it get *stronger* when you look over there?

Yeah, it *does*. Why?

Because I think I *know* where we are. We're still in the *gym*.

Is that meant to be *funny*, Paul?

I don't *do* jokes. I just state the *obvious* and make it sound funny.

Like, I might say, "You damn well *should* recognize this place--"

"--because you *made* it."

Ohhh, Christmas.

So here we *are*, babe. After all this *time*. I'm really *sorry* I hurt you, but that can't happen again.

I've anchored your *life* in mine, and mine in *yours*. We're joined at the *hip*.

You'll never *know* what I had to do to get you *back*.

I *squeezed* the Salem witches like ripe *zits* to get the magic out of them. I even *killed* some people. But that's in the past.

Nothing is *ever* gonna separate us now. And we don't have to *die*. We don't have to grow *old*.

I can give you *everything*. Everything you could want.

Chad--

You hurt my *friends*, and you scared the blanks.

You did a lot of *harm* that you can never put right.

You really think I'm going to *forgive* you for that?

GAAAHHHH!!

I've given *everything* for this!

And you--you're not even *grateful*. You don't even *care!*

I never *asked* you to kill me. I never asked you to bring me *back*.

I don't want *anything* you can give me, Chad.

Fine, then! Fine! I'll send you *back*, you crummy, freaky little-- *ghost*.

I'll-- I'll--

Nnnnuuuhhrrr I *can't.* I tied you to me!

I tied you to my *soul*. If you go, I go.

But hey, if you're so *worried* about your friends, and about the *blanks*--

--you can stand there and watch them *burn*, okay? Watch them crisp and burn and *fry*.

Okay. I'm going to need everything you've got, people. So I'll be shutting down some stuff that you *don't* need. Like *consciousness*.

We *made* it. Do your *stuff*, Foley.

Barrow! W--Wait! You can't do--make--go *ahead* with this.

Foley?

I'm in a really *bad* mood, man.

You remember what happened to *Knox*? Well *that's* the kind of mood I'm in.

I can-- I'm s--seeing how this *ends*. Something real--*bad* happens to you.

If I let you use my--my *sight*--will you s--set everybody *free*?

Let me use it?

Yeah. I mean if I *cooperate*. If I--*uuf!*

I don't *need* you to cooperate, you moron. I just *take*.

"Hey, Sally. How's it *going?*" "Not *good,* Kim."

"Can you *move?*"

"Only if Chad *tells* me to. He's got a *binding* spell on me."

"Well here's some late *news.* I'm a *necromancer*-- the dead are my thing."

"Even the *risen* dead. So give it to 'im, girl. You're *free.*"

"Now what is it you're *seeing,* Frankenfoley?"

"Let's take a *look.*"

"This is just like old *times,* Chad."

GUUUUH!

"Remember?"

Right, Sal. Are you *watching*? Now you're going to see Salem as I see it.

As a great big hole in the *ground*.

Chad.

No-- What, you want to say *sorry* now?

I want to say it's *over*.

Oww!

She's *told* me I can go. She's opened the *gate*.

And we're *one* now. Remember?

Joined at the *hip*.

Hey! Let *go* of me, you stupid little--

Let *go* of me!

End.